Smooth Collie Tricks Training

Smooth Collie Tricks & Games Training Tracker & Workbook.

Includes: Smooth Collie Multi-Level Tricks, Games & Agility.

Part 2

Training Central

Copyright © 2017

Introductory Note

Welcome to this interactive tricks workbook.

We want to start by thanking all of the Smooth Collie fans out there whom inspired us to complete this three part series in which we cover a variety of tricks and games that you can teach your pooch.

Our intention is for you to learn and grow with your beloved pup whilst having a great time. We trust that you will enjoy and benefit from the use of the books in this series.

Be sure to make notes on the pages found after each trick. We found this supports learning significantly.

Have fun whilst you log and note down your progress, any new ideas, thoughts, techniques that work for you/new methods, or even sketches.

Good luck and wishing you all the best.

Table of Contents

Preventing Jumps..4

Release..7

Drop It..10

Train Your Smooth Collie To Ring A Bell When He Needs To Go Outside..13

Leap Over a Stick..16

Shake Hands..19

High Five..22

Wave Hello..25

Speak..28

Quiet..31

Take a Bow..34

Spin..37

Give a Kiss..40

Roll Over..43

Beg..46

Play Dead..49

Counting Dog..52

Object Recognition..55

Directed Jumping..58

Pick a Card From a Deck..61

Preventing Jumps

Jumping is normal behavior for curious, overeager Smooth Collie puppies especially when they want attention. While this kind of behavior can be seen as adorable in the beginning, it can get annoying and frustrating especially if you have guests around.

To stop or prevent jumps just follow these simple steps:

1. Turn your back on him and say "Off".

2. The natural reaction of your pup would be to continue following you around in order to get your attention. Continue to keep your back turned as you say "off". When he obeys you and stops jumping, praise him, give him a treat, and ask him to sit. Keep in mind that when you praise your puppy, use a calm voice otherwise showing excitement may cause him to jump again.

3. He will realize that jumping will not earn him any attention and that sitting does. The key for succeeding here is to remain consistent. If your pup approaches you with a wagging tail but sits down, go ahead and praise him.

How did you get on? *What challenges did you face & how did you overcome them?* What could you do better for next time? **Any new discoveries?** Funny moments? *Memorable Photos?* **Sketches?**

Any other thoughts, comments or feedback

Release

Playing fetch can be a fun, relaxing activity for both you and your Smooth Collie while giving him exercise. Teaching your pup how to give you back his toy will really support your fetch training:

1. Use the bait and switch method where you throw his favorite toy first. Once he gets it, call him by his name to get his attention. When he turns to you, throw a second toy in a direction different from where you threw the first. He will drop the first toy in order to fetch the second.

2. When he is fetching the second toy, go get his first toy. Call your pup's name and repeat the method from the beginning. While he may see this as a chasing game, you are actually teaching him to come back to you.

3. After a few rounds throw the first toy again. Call your Smooth Collie by his name but do not throw the second toy just yet. As he approaches you with the first toy in his mouth, instruct him to "drop it" while showing him the second toy. As soon as he drops the first toy this is your cue to throw the second toy. When he starts running toward the second toy, get the first one and repeat the process.

4. After some time your Smooth Collie will learn to give back his toy to you after each time that you throw it, eliminating the need for a second toy.

Training your Smooth Collie to release an object from his mouth will not only come in handy for playing fetch, but it can also save his life. If for example he picks up a poisonous object or one that can choke him such as a rock, having him release at your command could be life saving.

How did you get on? *What challenges did you face & how did you overcome them?* What could you do better for next time? **Any new discoveries?** Funny moments? *Memorable Photos?* **Sketches?**

Any other thoughts, comments or feedback

Drop It

The command "drop it" will stop your Smooth Collie from holding onto hazardous objects. The objective of this method is to reward him when he lets go of an object from his mouth.

1. Gather objects that your Smooth Collie is fond of chewing on. Have a few food treats ready in one hand which you will use as you tempt your pup to chew on an object.

2. When he puts the object in his mouth, use the "drop it" command as you put the treat closer to his nose, encouraging him to let go of the object.

3. Use your other hand to pick up the object as you praise him and continue feeding him. Return the object to your pup and practice this command a few more times.

If you don't succeed in making your Smooth Collie pick up another object, this is fine. Practice every day whenever he puts an object in his mouth, using the "drop it" command until he understands it.

Next, teach your puppy to drop the object using a tasty chew item.

1. Hold one end of the tasty chew while offering the other end to your pup.

2. As soon as he puts it into his mouth, command him to "drop it" as you pretend to offer him another treat.

3. On his first attempt, reward him with 3 treats and repeat. If he refuses to cooperate, hide the tasty chew and practice again the next day until he eventually learns to drop the object even when you are holding it.

4. The next task is to teach your pup to "drop it" using delicious chews such as cheese or meat that are cut up in small cubes. Use the "drop it" command as you show him a treat. As soon as he drops the object give him several cubes and let him keep the object instead of taking it away. Show him the treat first if he refuses to drop the chews. If this doesn't work, replace the chew with something that isn't as tasty. This process will allow you to develop your practice using more valuable objects.

5. Eventually you can try this exercise using items found around your home that your puppy may be inclined to chew on. Try it out with shoes, wrappers, or children's toys. You can also try it outdoors with rocks, sticks, leaves, and other objects that you can find at the park or in your yard. In the event that your Smooth Collie does put a hazardous item in his mouth and refuses to drop it, pull his mouth open using your hands and manually remove the object. After each "drop it" exercise always be sure to reward him.

How did you get on? *What challenges did you face & how did you overcome them?* What could you do better for next time? **Any new discoveries?** Funny moments?
Memorable Photos? **Sketches?**
Any other thoughts, comments or feedback

Train Your Smooth Collie To Ring A Bell When He Needs To Go Outside

Tricks are fun and practicing them can help deepen the relationship with your Smooth Collie while impressing onlookers. As you progress with teaching your pup tricks, you may want to consider purchasing a clicker to help speed up training.

For this trick, you will need to have a clicker, bell, and treats. Apart from being entertaining this can also come in handy as an additional command for house training. When you teach him to use a bell, you will be able to hear it so you will know he has to go outside. Young puppies don't have the ability to communicate with their owners to tell them that they need to go out.

1. Have a stick in hand for the bell.

2. Each time your Smooth Collie touches the bell, click and offer him a treat.

3. When your pup touches the bell on his own, click it and let him out then offer him a treat.

4. Once your Smooth Collie is outside, use the stick to lead him to the bell. His reward this time will be to open the door.

5. In a few days, he will learn that touching the bell will lead him to an open door.

How did you get on? *What challenges did you face & how did you overcome them?* What could you do better for next time? **Any new discoveries?** Funny moments?

Memorable Photos? **Sketches?**

Any other thoughts, comments or feedback

Leap Over a Stick

Teaching your Smooth Collie to leap over objects is one of the most impressive tricks you can teach him. In fact it is a trick used commonly in dog shows. Before you start with this command, check with your vet if jumping is safe for your Smooth Collie. Keep in mind that teaching puppies to leap isn't a good idea because it may damage their hips; it is best to teach this trick when your Smooth Collie is over 1.5 years of age. If your Smooth Collie has had hip dysplasia, skip this one altogether. For this trick you will need a clicker, treats, 2 chairs, a broom, and books.

1. Instruct your pup to sit and stay as you put a stick on the floor.

2. Walk over to the other side of the stick then call your Smooth Collie by his name.

3. When he crosses over to where you are, use the clicker and offer him a treat.

4. Repeat this several times after which you can add to the height by using books.

5. Each time your Smooth Collie crosses the stick and books, use the clicker and treat.

6. When he gets used to it, make it more challenging by adding even more books. When the books get high enough that he needs to leap over them, begin using the word "leap" followed by clicking then give him a treat and praise him. Repeat this until your Smooth Collie learns to leap on command.

How did you get on? *What challenges did you face & how did you overcome them?* What could you do better for next time? **Any new discoveries?** Funny moments? *Memorable Photos?* **Sketches?**

Any other thoughts, comments or feedback

Shake Hands

One way that your Smooth Collie can truly display good manners is by having the ability to shake hands. This is a traditional trick. Before you begin, pick a phrase that works with you and be consistent in using it. Some owners like "give me paw" while others prefer "shake hands".

1. Ask your Smooth Collie to sit and when he does, grab a paw, shake it, and let go.

2. Use the clicker or praise him generously then give him a treat. Repeat this exercise several times.

3. The next goal of this exercise is to have your Smooth Collie give you his paw instead of you grabbing it. Do this by gently tapping on his foot. If he is a quick learner he will know to give you his paw as soon as your hand approaches his foot.

4. Immediately reward him when he gives you his paw.

5. If your Smooth Collie doesn't give you his paw simply go back to step one and repeat the exercise.

6. Make sure that he is in a comfortable place while you teach him how to shake hands. Use only one command during training to avoid confusion; you want your pup to learn all tricks as fast as possible.

How did you get on? *What challenges did you face & how did you overcome them?* What could you do better for next time? **Any new discoveries?** Funny moments?

Memorable Photos? **Sketches?**

Any other thoughts, comments or feedback

High Five

High five is a similar trick to shaking hands. The only difference is that your hand is in a higher position. It should be easy to teach this trick once your Smooth Collie has learnt how to shake hands.

1. Command him to sit down, then ask him to shake hands.

2. Keep your hand higher, just on the same level as his head.

3. Practice this exercise until your Smooth Collie succeeds in giving you a high five.

4. Make it challenging by switching paws as you train him to master the high five trick.

How did you get on? *What challenges did you face & how did you overcome them?* What could you do better for next time? **Any new discoveries?** Funny moments?
Memorable Photos? **Sketches?**
Any other thoughts, comments or feedback

Wave Hello

Once you have successfully taught your Smooth Collie how to shake hands and give a high five, it should be relatively easy to teach him how to wave.

1. Command him to go into a sitting position.

2. Use the high five command several times so that your Smooth Collie gets used to the paw shake each time you hold out your hand.

3. Put your hand in the same position as the "high five" so that he understands you want him to do this trick again.

4. When you see him raising his paw towards your hand, put your hand down. Once he notices that you pulled your hand away, he will put his paw back down after which you should praise and treat him.

5. Soon your Smooth Collie will learn the trick and may wave several times in a row. Keep practicing this command until he understands how to wave.

How did you get on? *What challenges did you face & how did you overcome them?* What could you do better for next time? **Any new discoveries?** Funny moments?

Memorable Photos? **Sketches?**

Any other thoughts, comments or feedback

Speak

Teaching your Smooth Collie to speak or bark on command is useful in helping him learn when it is appropriate to bark. This command may prove challenging if your Smooth Collie is naturally calm but remains patient.

1. Get your Smooth Collie excited by playing games with him or chasing him around.

2. Once he is excited get him ready for training. Hold a treat in one hand and show it to him. If he already knows several tricks by this point, he may attempt doing several of them to get the treat, or he may get frustrated and end up whining.

3. Move the treat around and tease him by waving the treat in front of his face; the goal of this activity is to encourage him to bark.

4. When he does bark, say the command "speak" and then hand him a treat. By this time your Smooth Collie won't understand what just happened, but practice the trick again as he figures out the behavior you want from him. As he gets frustrated he will bark again but if he doesn't, begin by getting him excited again.

5. Generously praise and reward him when he does bark at your command.

6. Keep repeating the command "speak" until he makes sounds regardless if it is howling or barking. Immediately praise and treat him each time he speaks.

7. Continue repeating the exercise until your Smooth Collie associates "speak" with this trick. Command practices for "speak" should last 10-15 minutes. The goal is to get him frustrated enough to make a sound and reward him as soon as he does.

How did you get on? *What challenges did you face & how did you overcome them?* What could you do better for next time? **Any new discoveries?** Funny moments? *Memorable Photos?* **Sketches?**

Any other thoughts, comments or feedback

Quiet

Quiet is a very useful command to calm down your Smooth Collie when he makes noises. It is also logical to teach this trick after he has mastered "speak". This command will also teach him the appropriate time he can bark.

1. Command your Smooth Collie to "speak", and when he does, say "quiet".

2. Once he stops barking praise him and give him a treat.

3. At this point your Smooth Collie may be confused because you are using two commands simultaneously. But to make it clearer for him, try this command when he is barking at something outside. If he stops barking then you know he understands the command.

4. Continue practicing this command and repeat "quiet" every time he stops barking, then reward him.

Keep in mind to only say the word "quiet" when he stops barking. He will probably ignore you if you instruct him as he is barking. Continue practicing this trick so that you can use it while he is barking when he has fully mastered it.

How did you get on? *What challenges did you face & how did you overcome them?* What could you do better for next time? **Any new discoveries?** Funny moments? *Memorable Photos?* **Sketches?**

Any other thoughts, comments or feedback

Take a Bow

With this trick your Smooth Collie will learn to execute a "bowing" stance where he leans forward using his elbows as his chest touches the ground. This command is a great finishing touch after he has performed several entertaining tricks.

1. With your Smooth Collie standing up, hold a food treat right by his nose.

2. Gradually move it down as you keep it close to his body as a way of luring him down until his elbows touch the floor while his back side is standing upright.

3. Once he gets into the desired bow pose position, have him maintain it for a few seconds. Get another food treat to lure him back into the standing position.

4. When he completes the bow pose and is already standing, praise and reward him.

5. Practice this command three times a day, for 5 minutes each. Soon enough your Smooth Collie will be able to master the "take a bow" command.

In the beginning, it is common for most Smooth Collies to experience difficulty keeping their rear in the air as they learn this trick. To encourage your pup to keep it up longer you can place your arm under his stomach while using your other hand to lure his upper half down.

How did you get on? *What challenges did you face & how did you overcome them?* What could you do better for next time? **Any new discoveries?** Funny moments?

Memorable Photos? **Sketches?**

Any other thoughts, comments or feedback

Spin

Spinning is a fun and entertaining trick that's also easy to teach.

1. Start out with your Smooth Collie in the standing position then hold a treat in front of his nose as you instruct him to "spin".

2. Put the treat on the side of his nose slowly, encouraging him to follow it as he turns his head to the side.

3. Pull the treat in a circle around his body so that he will need to move into a spinning motion to keep track of it.

4. When your Smooth Collie has gone round in a complete circle, praise and reward him.

5. Practice the spin command every day for at least 5 minutes.

How did you get on? *What challenges did you face & how did you overcome them?* What could you do better for next time? **Any new discoveries?** Funny moments? *Memorable Photos?* **Sketches?**
Any other thoughts, comments or feedback

Give a Kiss

Who wouldn't like to be given kisses on command by their canine companions? This trick is one of the best out there since you'll be able to easily ask for affection from your Smooth Collie anytime you want to. For this trick, have some delicious edible treats. I recommend cream cheese or some peanut butter since it's easy to smear these on your hand or cheeks.

1. Place a small dab of cream cheese or peanut butter on your hand or cheek.

2. Instruct your Smooth Collie to "give kisses".

3. Approach him and let him do the rest; he should then learn to lick the treat from you.

4. Practice the "give kisses" command several times throughout the day until he masters it.

5. Offer praises and rewards generously whenever he learns to kiss you on command.

To speed up learning this trick, you can also help him by capturing his behavior. Simply give the command "give kisses" whenever he licks you.

How did you get on? *What challenges did you face & how did you overcome them?* What could you do better for next time? **Any new discoveries?** Funny moments? *Memorable Photos?* **Sketches?**

Any other thoughts, comments or feedback

Roll Over

Before you teach your Smooth Collie the roll over command, be sure that he has already mastered the down and sit command. This trick may be more challenging to teach but with patience and practice he should be able to pick it up in a week or two. Clicker training will contribute more effectively in training the roll over trick to your Smooth Collie.

1. Give him the "down" command and once he has successfully obeyed your command proceed to step 2.

2. Use a food treat and hold it by his nose. Slowly use the treat to lure his nose towards his shoulder. By this time your Smooth Collie should be able to move his head in order to follow the treat.

3. When he moves his head, continue using the treat to lure him around his shoulder so that he is required to lie down sideways to follow it.

4. Holding the treat close to his nose, continue pulling it around so he needs to do a complete roll over.

5. Upon completing a complete roll over, generously praise your Smooth Collie and use the clicker then reward him with a treat.

If you find that your pup tends to make several mistakes as he learns the "roll over" trick, you may be doing it too quickly. All you need to do is move back to the stage when he was doing well, then start again but more slowly this time around. You may find that he is hesitant to expose his belly but remind him that it's just for fun by giving him a playful belly rub while using a positive and uplifting tone of voice.

How did you get on? *What challenges did you face & how did you overcome them?* What could you do better for next time? **Any new discoveries?** Funny moments?
Memorable Photos? **Sketches?**
Any other thoughts, comments or feedback

Beg

This fun trick will teach your Smooth Collie how to beg on command.

1. To start the training ask him to follow the sit command.

2. Once he is sitting, use a food treat and hold it in front of his nose while giving the "beg" command.

3. The natural instinct of your Smooth Collie will be to attempt to take the treat from your hand. When he does this, raise the treat above his head so he will need to move up to get it.

4. Continue pulling it up so that he ends up sitting on his rear end and his front paws are off the floor. Once he is in this position hold the treat in front of him. He is now successfully in the "beg" position; reward him and use the clicker.

5. Repeat the steps to mastering the "beg" position several times per day until he has mastered it.

How did you get on? *What challenges did you face & how did you overcome them?* What could you do better for next time? **Any new discoveries?** Funny moments?
Memorable Photos? **Sketches?**
Any other thoughts, comments or feedback

Play Dead

This is a great trick for showing off to guests just how well trained your Smooth Collie is. It's pretty easy to teach him how to play dead, just follow the simple steps below.

1. Start the training by commanding your Smooth Collie to go into the "down" position.

2. Choose what command you'd like to use to instruct your pup to play dead; some people like to use the verbal cue "bang" or simply "play dead" accompanied by a hand signal where you imitate a gun pointing at your pup.

3. When you say the verbal cue, hold up a treat next to his nose. Gradually move the treat to the side so that he will need to roll sideways to reach it. This trick should be easy if your Smooth Collie has already mastered the "roll over" trick.

4. As soon as he is lying on his side, let him know that he is doing the right thing by praising him or using the clicker, followed by a treat.

5. Continue practicing this command by instructing him to roll over several times throughout the day. Soon enough he will roll over when you use the hand signal combined with the verbal cue.

For dogs that have already mastered how to "roll over" they may end up rolling over completely. In this instance a clicker can come in handy to communicate to exactly the behavior you are expecting of him. Use a treat to lure him to his side then immediately use the clicker followed by a tasty treat. If your Smooth Collie continues to roll over, take a step back and once he sees that the treat has disappeared each time he does this, he will start carrying out the behavior that only leads to a treat.

How did you get on? *What challenges did you face & how did you overcome them?* What could you do better for next time? **Any new discoveries?** Funny moments? *Memorable Photos?* **Sketches?**
Any other thoughts, comments or feedback

Counting Dog

1. Command your Smooth Collie to sit facing you.

2. Place a treat in your left hand while your right hand is held up. During this step you are trying to get him to associate the speaking command together with the visual command of your right hand up. Perform this step while looking at your Smooth Collie straight in the eye.

3. Command him to "Speak" and when he does, give him a treat.

4. Repeat step 3, only this time drop your right hand and only offer the treat when your Smooth Collie barks twice.

5. Repeat this trick several times until he understands that he is being asked to bark until your hand drops.

6. As you progress through training, gradually eliminate the use of your right hand up so that your pup will learn to associate the cue to stop speaking with eye contact instead.

7. Keep practicing until your Smooth Collie learns to respond with a smooth progression of barks and stops when you halt eye contact.

How did you get on? *What challenges did you face & how did you overcome them?* What could you do better for next time? **Any new discoveries?** Funny moments?

Memorable Photos? **Sketches?**

Any other thoughts, comments or feedback

Object Recognition

1. Before you start training, think of how you would like your Smooth Collie to indicate an object to you. You can choose from: using a paw, nose target, mouth target, or looking at it.

2. Start with one object, point at it and name it before he indicates it.

3. Each time your Smooth Collie properly indicates the object, reward him with a treat.

4. After several sessions try saying the name of the object without pointing at it and see if he is able to indicate it without your help. Each time he is able to, give him a treat and move on to step 5.

5. Choose another object that has a different sounding name from the first object. It is recommended to use a second object that also looks very different from the first which will make it easier for your Smooth Collie. Choose an object name that doesn't sound similar to another object or cue that you've already used with your pup.

6. Point at the second object the first few times but fade it quickly. Follow the reward process where you treat him every time he gets it right.

7. Next, alternate two objects in your training until he can clearly identify the difference between both objects using your verbal cues.

How did you get on? *What challenges did you face & how did you overcome them?* What could you do better for next time? **Any new discoveries?** Funny moments?

Memorable Photos? **Sketches?**

Any other thoughts, comments or feedback

Directed Jumping

1. Set up 2 bar jumps side by side.

2. Command your Smooth Collie to stay in front of one of them.

3. Place yourself on the other side of the bar jump and call your pup over. Repeat this with the other jump.

4. When your Smooth Collie is in front of one of the jumps, challenge him by placing yourself between both jumps.

5. Signal him by raising your arm closest to one jump. You may use a toy or treat bag in the beginning to get his attention.

6. Continue practicing on this command until he can obey commands while both of you are centered between jumps. Combine verbal and hand signals to communicate where you want him to jump.

How did you get on? *What challenges did you face & how did you overcome them?* What could you do better for next time? **Any new discoveries?** Funny moments? *Memorable Photos?* **Sketches?**

Any other thoughts, comments or feedback

Pick a Card From a Deck

1. Hold one playing card in your hand and offer it to your Smooth Collie as you instruct him to "take it".

2. Take 3 cards and hold them in a fan and ask him to take one. Reward him when he obeys regardless of which card he takes.

3. Add a fourth card and extend one so that it's easier for your Smooth Collie to take it.

4. As you progress through the training, gradually reduce the card extension so he learns to pick one even if it does not stick out from the fan.

5. If your Smooth Collie pulls out two cards, simply put the cards back and try again.

6. When he has mastered the commands you can practice this with the entire deck as you hold them out but with a few cards extended slightly ahead of other cards.

How did you get on? *What challenges did you face & how did you overcome them?* What could you do better for next time? **Any new discoveries?** Funny moments? *Memorable Photos?* **Sketches?**

Any other thoughts, comments or feedback

Food Refusal

1. Have several treats available as you teach your Smooth Collie food refusal.

2. Command him to sit, and remain close to him throughout the training.

3. Hold a treat up in front of your Smooth Collie; this will entice him to move as an attempt to take the treat. During his attempt, pull away the treat and say "No!".

4. If he uses his nose to gently touch the food, this is when you can offer him the treat. Reinforce the positive behavior by praising and petting him.

5. Gradually delay the interval between treats. Your Smooth Collie should be able to resist treats and instead gently touch your hand using his nose. When he does this, reward him and reinforce positive behavior.

6. Eventually he will develop his behavior and will no longer attempt to snatch food. Upon reaching this point, try this trick while placing food on your hand wide open.

7. If your Smooth Collie attempts to jump or snatch the snack on your palm, close it and move back.

8. If he behaves by resisting food and sitting down, praise him and give a reward.

How did you get on? *What challenges did you face & how did you overcome them?* What could you do better for next time? **Any new discoveries?** Funny moments? *Memorable Photos?* **Sketches?**

Any other thoughts, comments or feedback

Find the Object With My Scent

1. Command your Smooth Collie to sit in front of you.

2. Place an object that he is familiar with in front of him, and have him sniff it.

3. Put the item under a towel or a pillow and ask him to "find it". You can give the object a name, such as "toy", then combine it with the command such as "Find it toy".

4. Click and reward him when he touches the item with his nose or paw.

5. Repeat steps 1-4 several times but place the object on different locations, challenging your Smooth Collie even more.

6. Change it up as your pup progresses by asking him to smell other objects that he is less familiar with and asking him to find it.

How did you get on? *What challenges did you face & how did you overcome them?* What could you do better for next time? **Any new discoveries?** Funny moments?

Memorable Photos? **Sketches?**

Any other thoughts, comments or feedback

Contraband Search

Bring out your pup's prey drive by playing ball or tug of war. During contraband or a narcotics search, dogs must be in prey drive.

Store the ball with pseudo contraband so that the ball has the same smell as the contraband. When your Smooth Collie plays with the ball he will learn to associate it with the contraband.

1. Halt the game before he is through playing as this will have him excited and wanting more.

2. Place the ball under your foot and encourage him to try and fetch it.

3. Release the ball if your Smooth Collie scratches as an attempt to get it. This will encourage the scratching indication and build up his drive even more.

4. Practice this trick by hiding the ball in various locations such as the garage where he can see the ball and scratch to get it.

5. As the training progresses, hide the ball in a place where he can only see the ball but is unable to get it through scratching. The scent of the contraband should still be on the ball or at least in the location of the ball. By this time you can train him to have two alerts; either scratch and sit, or aggressively scratch the board. If you opt for the scratch and sit you must command him to sit after he scratches.

6. Practice contraband search when your Smooth Collie is off leash, ensuring that he is in a safe place and remains in prey drive.

7. Place an emphasis on ensuring he has fun as he locates the ball so that when you move up to advanced training in more complex locations his goal will be on finding the ball without the leash. If your Smooth Collie has a hard time focusing without a leash, keep it on.

8. Hide the ball in a place where the visibility is hidden from your pup, such as in the crate or in the car exterior.

9. Wait for him to give off alerts that he is excited by the scent. Since the contraband is hidden you can remove the ball from the hide location provided that it is still hidden with the contraband.

10. Make sure that the ball is with the contraband until you have covered various training set-ups.

11. When the contraband is visually hidden, your Smooth Collie will be challenged to find it; at this point you can pretend to look for it with him by sniffing around but avoid finding the contraband for him. Eventually he will be more interested in searching for it.

12. Next, transition your training by switching to vehicles and do a dry run of the search as your pup watches.

13. Have him check the entire vehicle as you hide the contraband in various locations.

14. Use the point to point method to develop his drive; this method is best used on several vehicles. Go from one point in the car and look at it, followed by another point and so on as your Smooth Collie watches.

15. Have him search by giving the command "check here"

16. Continue the training until he has mastered the contraband search.

How did you get on? What challenges did you face & how did you overcome them? What could you do better for next time? Any new discoveries? Funny moments? Memorable Photos? Sketches?
Any other thoughts, comments or feedback

Track a Person's Scent Trail

1. The easiest way to begin teaching your Smooth Collie to track a person's scent trail is by laying it on moist grass. Rub your feet at the beginning which creates a "scent pad" and continue doing this for the next 50 yards as you walk in a straight line.

2. Drop treats that have a strong odor such as small cuts of meat every few yards.

3. Use flags to mark your trail then leave an object marked with your scent at the end of it. You can use a simple object such as a sock stuffed with treats to heighten his interest.

4. Place a harness on your Smooth Collie as you lead him to the scent pad. Give him the command to "track" and encourage him to find the first treat on your trail. Gently use the harness if he pulls you off course.

5. Once he finds the first object train him to provide a signal by lying down. He should continue doing this until he reaches the end of the trail and finds your sock, after which he should also lie down. Reward him with some treats from the sock to reinforce positive behavior.

6. Repeat this until your Smooth Collie has mastered how to track your scent trail.

7. The trail will have your scent for the next several days so to advance the training you may use a different location.

How did you get on? *What challenges did you face & how did you overcome them?* What could you do better for next time? **Any new discoveries?** Funny moments?
Memorable Photos? **Sketches?**
Any other thoughts, comments or feedback

Heel Forward and Backward

1. Hold your Smooth Collie on a loose leash on your left side.

2. Command him to "heel" as you walk forward using your left foot first, keeping in mind that this will eventually be his cue to heel. Verbal commands should come first before the action.

3. Reward and praise him every time his shoulder is by your left leg.

4. Gradually stop by slowing your walk, then place your left foot firmly on the ground, and align it with your right foot.

5. Pull the leash and command your Smooth Collie to "sit".

6. Use your right foot to gently tap his chest and say the command "back".

7. When he takes a step back give him a reward ensuring that it's right in front of him so he doesn't have to move forward to get it. For quicker learning you may want to practice this trick against the wall to help keep him straight.

How did you get on? *What challenges did you face & how did you overcome them?* What could you do better for next time? **Any new discoveries?** Funny moments?

Memorable Photos? **Sketches?**

Any other thoughts, comments or feedback

Back Up

1. Stand as you face your Smooth Collie, and hold a treat in a closed fist as you place it in front of his nose.

2. Gently press his nose as you walk toward him and give him the command to "scoot".

3. When your Smooth Collie moves backwards, praise and reward him.

4. If he doesn't move back, use a foot to guide him on his side.

5. Eventually your Smooth Collie will get used to this command then you can gradually eliminate the use of nose pressing. Instead, give him cues by walking toward him as you raise your knee to gently tap his chest.

6. Use your hand to give him signals to move backward.

7. As you progress through practice, use smaller steps backwards but continue to raise your knee to cue your Smooth Collie to go back. Give him rewards or toss it to him so he won't need to move forward to you to obtain it.

How did you get on? *What challenges did you face & how did you overcome them?* What could you do better for next time? **Any new discoveries?** Funny moments?
Memorable Photos? **Sketches?**
Any other thoughts, comments or feedback

Take a Bow

1. Command your Smooth Collie to stand as he faces you. In your hand, have a treat which you will hold up toward his nose.

2. Gently push your hand to his nose then downward followed by a verbal cue.

3. When his elbows touch the floor, give him a treat then take your hand away.

4. Continue to repeat until fluent.

How did you get on? *What challenges did you face & how did you overcome them?* What could you do better for next time? **Any new discoveries?** Funny moments?
Memorable Photos? **Sketches?**
Any other thoughts, comments or feedback

Place (Circle To My Left Side)

1. Face your Smooth Collie as you stand up, holding his leash on your right hand.

2. Use the command "place" then step your right foot back as you pull him toward your right then coaxing him to go behind you. Keep your left foot firmly on the ground all throughout the training.

3. Put the leash on your left hand then put your right foot beside your left. Gently use the leash to pull your Smooth Collie to your left side.

4. Pull the leash then command him to sit; reward and praise your Smooth Collie when he obeys.

How did you get on? *What challenges did you face & how did you overcome them?* What could you do better for next time? **Any new discoveries?** Funny moments?
Memorable Photos? **Sketches?**
Any other thoughts, comments or feedback

Walk On Your Left or Right Side

1. Use a touch stick to command your Smooth Collie to go around your right side then stand at your left. Click and treat to show him that this is the desired behavior.

2. Continue this step as you use "left" as a verbal cue when he goes to your left side.

3. Repeat until your Smooth Collie no longer relies on the touch stick and will go to either side upon hearing your verbal command.

4. Do the same until your Smooth Collie masters the trick on both sides.

How did you get on? *What challenges did you face & how did you overcome them?* What could you do better for next time? **Any new discoveries?** Funny moments?
Memorable Photos? **Sketches?**
Any other thoughts, comments or feedback

Leg Weave

1. Hold treats in your right hand while facing your Smooth Collie. As you stand, your legs should be shoulder width apart.

2. Slowly bend over then use your right hand to reach between your legs. Use the treat to get his attention as you coax him to move from your front to your back through your legs.

3. When your Smooth Collie obeys, praise and reward him as you say "Good boy! Weave!" so he is familiar with the verbal cue.

4. Repeat three times until his is used to the leg weave.

5. During the succeeding training session, prepare treats in both hands and repeat steps 1-3. When he circles your left leg and comes out up front, use your left hand to reach between your legs and pull him back.

6. Gently pull him around your left leg and then back up again in front of you. Praise and reward your Smooth Collie and give him a treat.

How did you get on? *What challenges did you face & how did you overcome them?* What could you do better for next time? **Any new discoveries?** Funny moments?

Memorable Photos? **Sketches?**

Any other thoughts, comments or feedback

Figure 8s

1. Have small treats ready in both hands.

2. Start practicing with your Smooth Collie standing on your left side, then hold a treat to his nose.

3. Slowly move the treat in your hand forward, and then between your legs.

4. When he reaches the side of your legs, give him a treat.

5. Gently coax him back to go between your legs.

6. Make both of your hands meet in the middle so that your Smooth Collie follows the new hand.

7. Lead him to your left side, then reward and praise him. Continue practicing until your Smooth Collie perform the figure 8s.

How did you get on? *What challenges did you face & how did you overcome them?* What could you do better for next time? **Any new discoveries?** Funny moments? *Memorable Photos?* **Sketches?**

Any other thoughts, comments or feedback

Moonwalk

1. Sit down as you face your Smooth Collie and lure him downwards using a treat.

2. When he is down, place the treat right under his nose.

3. When your Smooth Collie begins to follow the treat, slowly move it towards his chest. He should back up to obtain the treat. As soon as he begins moving backwards, immediately use a clicker or praise him then give him the treat.

4. As he learns to back up quicker when he sees your hand approaching him, attempt the trick without a lure. Your Smooth Collie should be able to move backwards even without the food lure but if he doesn't, simply use the treat again as a lure and attempt the trick again.

5. Begin fading the use of your hand signal and opt for verbal cues such as scoot, back, or crawl.

How did you get on? *What challenges did you face & how did you overcome them?* What could you do better for next time? **Any new discoveries?** Funny moments? *Memorable Photos?* **Sketches?**

Any other thoughts, comments or feedback

Jump

1. Have some small treats hidden in your back pocket.

2. Call your Smooth Collie and order him to sit.

3. Pull one treat out of your pocket and show it to your Smooth Collie by holding it in front of his nose.

4. Gradually pull the treat higher around a foot or two above him.

5. Give him the verbal command to "jump" and with the treat still in your hand, demonstrate the jump yourself while repeating "jump".

6. When your Smooth Collie catches on and begins imitating your jump, praise and reward him.

How did you get on? *What challenges did you face & how did you overcome them?* What could you do better for next time? **Any new discoveries?** Funny moments? *Memorable Photos?* **Sketches?**

Any other thoughts, comments or feedback

Dance

1. Start the practice by having your Smooth Collie face you as he sits down.

2. Show him a treat as you lure him onto his hind legs.

3. While he is still on his back legs, offer one treat and praise him.

4. Lure him to his hind legs as you continue giving him one treat after another. Continue praising him as he stands, gradually increasing the time he is on his back legs.

5. Use the verbal cue "dance" as you lead your Smooth Collie into position. Each time he obeys you, give a treat and enthusiastically praise him.

6. Hold treats in your left hand and use your right hand to signal so that your Smooth Collie will learn to stand even when you are not holding a treat.

7. If he learns to stay on his hind legs for several seconds, get a treat and lead him to a circle when he stands up. In the beginning you may only succeed with a part of a circle but continue being enthusiastic as you praise and treat him.

8. Eventually, his strength and muscles will develop to master this trick and he will be able to complete a full circle.

How did you get on? *What challenges did you face & how did you overcome them?* What could you do better for next time? **Any new discoveries?** Funny moments?

Memorable Photos? **Sketches?**

Any other thoughts, comments or feedback

Fetch Slippers

1. Use the "take it" trick and train your Smooth Collie to bring you slippers.

2. Give him a few minutes to sniff the slippers, familiarize himself with the object and the verbal cue for it.

3. Command your Smooth Collie to take it and bring it to you. When he obeys, use the clicker and enthusiastically praise him and offer him a treat.

4. Tell him to "Bring my slippers", and if he obeys you, click, praise and reward him.

How did you get on? *What challenges did you face & how did you overcome them?* What could you do better for next time? **Any new discoveries?** Funny moments?

Memorable Photos? **Sketches?**

Any other thoughts, comments or feedback

Get the Leash

1. Place the leash on the floor then instruct your Smooth Collie to "take it". When he obeys, use the clicker and give him a food treat.

2. Walk toward the door and command him to take the leash then place it on your hands using the command "drop it". Use the clicker once he obeys, then reward him.

3. Reduce the verbal commands and stick to "leash"; if he is slow to pick it up you can use hand signals to offer a hint.

4. Instruct him to get the leash and when he follows the command, take him out for a walk as a reward.

How did you get on? *What challenges did you face & how did you overcome them?* What could you do better for next time? **Any new discoveries?** Funny moments? *Memorable Photos?* **Sketches?**

Any other thoughts, comments or feedback

Bring You a Tissue

1. Place a tissue box on the floor then command your Smooth Collie to "take it". He may attempt to take the entire tissue box but if he manages to only pull one out, click then treat.

2. Continue doing this until he learns to pull out tissues on his own. Use the "bring it" and "drop it" commands so that he learns to bring the tissue and drop it on your hands.

3. Practice this trick until he follows your commands and then switch to the verbal cue "bring me a tissue" when he masters it.

How did you get on? *What challenges did you face & how did you overcome them?* What could you do better for next time? **Any new discoveries?** Funny moments?
Memorable Photos? **Sketches?**
Any other thoughts, comments or feedback

Newspaper Delivery

1. Throw a newspaper across the room and have your Smooth Collie watch you do this. He should already be familiar with fetching by this time, and he should automatically get it and bring it back to you.

2. Each time he brings the newspaper to you, be enthusiastic and praise him, offer him treats as well.

3. Next, practice the trick outdoors. Start by throwing it at a similar area. Reward him each time he brings you the newspaper.

4. Choose a specific verbal cue to signal that you want him to get the newspaper and don't use this cue for any other trick. For example, yell "Paper!" so he associates it with this command.

5. When your Smooth Collie is indoors, go outside and leave the paper there; then let him out and give the command. Since you didn't throw it for him, he should get used to going out and finding it. If your Smooth Collie doesn't catch on the first few times, accompany him outside to show him where to go.

6. When he gets used to going out and fetching the paper, challenge him by hiding it so it also becomes more fun for him. Be patient if it takes your Smooth Collie a while to learn this trick; keep in mind that it should be kept fun.

7. Practice daily by using the "paper" command, being consistent at all times. Eventually he will get the hang of it and will learn to fetch it when the newspaper is dropped off.

How did you get on? *What challenges did you face & how did you overcome them?* What could you do better for next time? **Any new discoveries?** Funny moments?
Memorable Photos? **Sketches?**
Any other thoughts, comments or feedback

Saying Prayers

1. Sit in a chair as you command your Smooth Collie to go into the sitting position while facing you.

2. Place a treat between your legs as you sit.

3. Give the verbal command "pray" as you coax your Smooth Collie to put both paws on your chair while he remains seated.

4. Use the "leave it" verbal cue to tell him that he should not eat the treat. This is followed by the "pray" command so that he sticks his nose down to the treat located between his paws.

5. Say "Amen" then release the treat for your Smooth Collie as you praise him.

How did you get on? *What challenges did you face & how did you overcome them?* What could you do better for next time? **Any new discoveries?** Funny moments? *Memorable Photos?* **Sketches?**

Any other thoughts, comments or feedback

CPSIA information can be obtained
at www.ICGtesting.com
Printed in the USA
LVOW10s1138151217
559823LV00019B/1155/P

9 781526 952783